A GREAT GAME!

POKÉMON GO

BY ALEXANDER LOWE

NORWOOD HOUSE PRESS

Norwood House Press

For information regarding Norwood House Press, please visit our website at www.norwoodhousepress.com or call 866-565-2900.

Credits
Editor: Lauren Dupuis-Perez
Designer: Sara Radka
Fact Checker: Meghan Gottschall and Renae Gilles
Special thanks to Wendy Vogelgesang.

Photo Credits
Getty Images: Billy H.C. Kwok, 26, Brendon Thorne, 16, Carl Court, 19, David McNew, 8, Drew Angerer, 23, Fiona Goodall, 13, iStock Editorial/EnchantedFairy, 37, iStock Editorial/Wachiwit, 15, iStock Unreleased/jfmdesign, 17, iStock Unreleased/JianGang Wang, 35, Stringer/Joe Scarnici, 5; Newscom: AFLO/Yoshio Tsunoda, 40, dpa/Andrej Sokolow, 39, dpa/Federico Gambarini, 29, KRT, 7; Pixabay: 95C, 10, stux, 28, vinksy2002, 11; Shutterstock: Anson_18, Brilliantist Studio, 4, Carlos Antonio, 25, dekitateyo, 31, Ivan_Sabo, 20, Manintino, cover, 1, Matthew Corley, 3, pim pic, 42, pondrafee, 21, Sheryl Watson, 30, 33, small1, 27, Stoyan Yotov, 36

Library of Congress Cataloging-in-Publication Data
Names: Lowe, Alexander, author.
Title: Pokémon Go / By Alexander Lowe.
Description: Chicago : Norwood House Press, [2021] | Series: A great game! | Includes index. | Audience: Ages 8-10 | Audience: Grades 4-6 | Summary: "An introductory look at the game of Pokémon GO. Describes the history of the game, introduces the creators and innovators, highlights competitions, and provides insight about the game's future. Informational text for readers who are new to Pokémon GO, or are interested in learning more. Includes a glossary, index, and bibliography for further reading"—Provided by publisher.
Identifiers: LCCN 2020019355 (print) | LCCN 2020019356 (ebook) | ISBN 9781684508501 (hardcover) | ISBN 9781684046027 (paperback) | ISBN 9781684046065 (epub)
Subjects: LCSH: Pokémon (Game)—Juvenile literature. | Pokémon (Fictitious characters)—Juvenile literature.
Classification: LCC GV1469.35.P63 L69 2021 (print) | LCC GV1469.35.P63 (ebook) | DDC 794.8—dc23
LC record available at https://lccn.loc.gov/2020019355
LC ebook record available at https://lccn.loc.gov/2020019356

Hardcover ISBN: 978-1-68450-850-1
Paperback ISBN: 978-1-68404-602-7

Pokémon GO™ is a registered trademark of Nintendo of America, Inc.
This book is not associated with Pokémon GO™, Nintendo or any of its associated partners.

328N—072020
Manufactured in the United States of America in North Mankato, Minnesota.

Table of Contents

Catch Them All!

Winds howl. Dust swirls. A storm lurks on the horizon. But that will not stop a truly fearless Pokémon GO master.

As she stares at the dirt ahead, she sees what she has been looking for. The cobra Pokémon Arbok. It crawls toward her. Quickly, she reaches for something to catch it with.

Pokémon GO™

Sign up with

G GOOGLE

POKÉMON TRAINER CLUB

Privacy Policy

©2016 Niantic Inc.
©2016 Pokémon
©1995-2016 Nintendo / Creatures Inc. / GAME FRE...

Singer Jordin Sparks is one of many celebrity fans of Pokémon GO. ™

The master flings the Poké Ball forward and it hits Arbok. The ball shakes once. It shakes again. Then it comes to rest. Arbok is caught. This Pokémon GO master is one step closer to catching them all.

History of Pokémon GO

Pokémon GO is a popular **mobile** video game made by the Pokémon Company. It is based on characters called Pokémon. Pokémon are colorful, animal-like creatures. They are the stars of one of the most popular **franchises** in the world. In 1996, Nintendo released the first games based on Pokémon characters in Japan. The games were made for the Nintendo Game Boy. A trading card game based on the Pokémon characters was also released in 1996. Each card featured a different Pokémon. A Pokémon TV series followed in 1997.

The Pokémon games and products became so popular that a separate company was needed to manage them. Tsunekazu Ishihara worked on the development of the company's games in the early 1990s. He helped make the Pokémon trading cards. This was one of the early ways the franchise became popular. Ishihara formed the Pokémon Company in 1998. He has been the president of the Pokémon Company ever since.

DID YOU KNOW?

Ingress is a game that Niantic created before Pokémon GO. The Pokémon GO world was created based on locations in Ingress.

The first Pokémon games were designed to be played on handheld gaming devices.

Nintendo president Satoru Iwata wanted to create a video game that helped people become more active.

Nintendo continued to make other products. One was the Wii. It was developed by Satoru Iwata. He was a boss at Nintendo. He wanted to follow the tradition of Nintendo's great video games. But he also saw problems with video games. Some people complained that games make kids lazy. He designed games that could improve health. In 2006, Nintendo released the Wii under his leadership. The Wii system later influenced Pokémon GO. Many older people played with the Wii system. The same is true for Pokémon GO. About 31 percent of the game's players are over 30 years old.

In 2014, Satoru Iwata and Tsunekazu Ishihara had an idea for a new game. This idea would eventually become Pokémon GO. They released a version of the game as an April Fools' joke with the help of Google. Google put a video online showing Pokémon in the wild. The people in the video looked at them through their cell phones. Many people got excited about the idea.

DID YOU KNOW?
Junichi Masuda composed the music for Pokémon GO. Masuda says he drew his inspiration from Nintendo's classic game Super Mario Bros.

History of Pokémon GO: Time Line

1996
The first Pokémon games are released for Nintendo Game Boy with 151 unique "pocket monsters."

2006
Nintendo releases the Wii console, which is the first gaming system that requires physical movement to play most of the games.

2010
John Hanke forms a company within Google called Niantic. The company would later launch Pokémon GO.

2014
Niantic and Google launch a pretend game for April Fool's Day. It shows Pokémon in the Google Maps app and includes a video of people looking at Pokémon in the real world using their phones.

2015
Niantic becomes independent from Google, and Hanke starts developing Pokémon GO with the idea to get people moving and talking to others.

2017
The first Pokémon GO Fest is held. It is so successful that more Go Fests are planned for the future, as well as monthly gatherings called Pokémon GO Community Days.

Iwata and Ishihara were inspired by a game called Ingress. Ingress was an **augmented reality** (AR) game made by a company called Niantic. Niantic was founded by John Hanke. Hanke's first company was called Keyhole. This company made **interactive** maps. Keyhole was bought by Google. Hanke worked on many projects for Google. Most of these involved maps. He helped create Google Earth. Hanke then moved his focus to video games. He started Niantic in 2010. In 2015, the idea for Pokémon GO led to a partnership between Nintendo, Niantic, and the Pokémon Company.

Works of Art

Ken Sugimori is one of the most important people in Pokémon history. He did the art for all 151 original Pokémon. That group included some of the most famous Pokémon known today. Sugimori set the artistic tone for Pokémon GO. Even the Pokémon that came after the original 151 were based on his style. Pokémon GO's initial release was a return to the original 151. It allowed younger fans to focus on the characters that once made up the game. In this way, many learned about the Pokémon their parents loved.

Many people helped create Pokémon GO. Employees at both Nintendo and Niantic worked on it. Tsunekazu Ishihara was also involved in the game. He said Pokémon was most popular in the 1990s. But he felt Pokémon GO could make the franchise popular again.

The game was released in the United States in the summer of 2016. It had 21 million active users. It made $207 million in the first month. One year after its release, Pokémon GO had 5 million daily active users. About 65 million people were playing it each month. The first Pokémon GO Fest was held in Chicago, Illinois, in 2017. The **phenomenon** had swept across the country.

Wow Wii!

The Wii is the first popular system where the body was the controller. Players have to move around. They have to use more than their thumbs. Wii Fit was made to be more than a game. It was also a way for players to get in shape. This mission was important to Pokémon GO as well. Wii's creator thought that games could help people be more active. He was very passionate about this mission. This would help people improve their quality of life. Pokémon GO followed in the Wii's footsteps. It got people moving to play a game.

Pokémon GO is a game parents and kids can enjoy together.

DID YOU KNOW?

Ken Sugimori's drawings were inspired by animals he observed in zoos and aquariums. Next time you visit the zoo, see if you can spot any animals that look like your favorite Pokémon!

Pokémon GO Basics

Pokémon GO is an AR game. AR games combine the real world and video games. This game is only on mobile devices. Players have to go into the real world. They find Pokémon in neighborhoods and parks. This would not work on a normal **console**.

Gamers can hunt Pokémon anywhere, from fields in the country to busy city sidewalks.

Catching Pokémon is a great way to make new friends.

The game involves players trying to find Pokémon. There is a map within the app. It shows where these **virtual** creatures are. The players are called trainers. They train their Pokémon to make them stronger.

Trainers must move around to play the game. This is one way Pokémon GO was inspired by Nintendo's Wii. In 2016, Pokémon GO players around the world walked about 4.5 billion miles (8.7 billion km) playing the game.

Trainers have to walk to find new Pokémon and other items, such as eggs. Walking helps hatch eggs. They become Pokémon. Other items can help catch or improve Pokémon.

DID YOU KNOW?

Pokémon is short for "pocket monsters," the original name given to the colorful creatures.

PokéStops are an important part of the game. These are locations where players can get new items. Poké Balls are used to catch new Pokémon. Players throw a ball at a Pokémon. When the Pokémon is hit by the ball, it is captured. Trainers then gain more Poké Balls at PokéStops. Many players who live near a PokéStop consider themselves lucky. They don't have to go far to get new items.

Trainers can also collect special gifts at PokéStops. They can give these to friends in the game. Players can also train with friends in the game. This helps players get extra points.

On Your Feet

Pokémon GO is unique because walking is part of the game. Players walk to hatch eggs. They also have to walk to find and capture Pokémon. This helps players stay fit. A 2019 study compared Pokémon GO players with people who do not play the game. Pokémon GO players walked nearly 1 mile (1.6 km) more per day. Catching Pokémon can have great health benefits for players!

Playing Pokémon GO can help gamers improve their map skills, since they have to be good with directions to catch a Pokémon.

Players can view Pokémon in the wild using the satellite or map view on their smartphones.

Battling is another important part of the game. Players are split into teams. Those teams are called Valor, Mystic, and Instinct. Teams battle to capture gyms. Gyms are locations where Pokémon can battle each other. The battles are between the different teams. Players compete to have the best team. Trainers who spend more time catching Pokémon have stronger teams. They can get Pokémon with more hit points (HP). This makes them better at gym battles. The more points a Pokémon has, the longer it lasts in a battle.

Fan Favorites

Every Pokémon fan has a favorite character. Many of the original 151 Pokémon are among the most popular. Fans have been following and collecting the characters for more than 20 years. A 2019 fan survey asked more than 52,000 fans to vote for their favorite Pokémon. Charizard (pictured right), Gengar, Arcanine, and Bulbasaur were the top four. Although he is one of the most recognizable Pokémon, Pikachu did not even make the top 20!

During a battle, two Pokémon attack each other. The Pokémon have different moves. These moves are known as attacks. Some attacks are stronger than others. Many moves have to be learned. Each Pokémon has a different number of HP. When the HP are gone, a Pokémon faints. That Pokémon loses the battle.

The gyms were changed in 2017. The change made them more focused on teamwork. Six Pokémon can be stored in a gym. Each trainer can only store one Pokémon at a time. This change made a strong team more important. One good trainer cannot defend a gym alone. Niantic also made it so multiple players could team up to fight against a gym. More than one trainer can bring their best Pokémon. The team with the strongest Pokémon controls the gym.

DID YOU KNOW?

Pokémon GO started with the 151 original Pokémon characters. Players can now find a total of 640 Pokémon in the game.

More than one person can catch the same Pokémon, so teaming up with a friend is a great way to play the game.

Pokémon GO Events

The Pokémon GO **community** is very important. This community includes all the players who play the game. The game has been **collaborative** from the start. That means that players work together. When a Pokémon is found, more than one player can catch it. Many players can catch Pokémon from the same location. This leads to friends and strangers playing together. They can tell others where new and rare Pokémon can be found.

DID YOU KNOW?

One of the first unofficial Pokémon GO events was held in 2016 in San Francisco, California. The organizers were expecting a few hundred people, but more than 9,000 players showed up to catch Pokémon!

Special Pokémon GO events attract large groups of people who want a shot at hunting unique Pokémon.

Some Pokémon GO trainers are so dedicated to catching Pokémon that they play the game at night.

There is some competition in hunting for Pokémon. Not all Pokémon can be found everywhere. Rare ones can only be found in certain places. Players want to be the first to find Pokémon. The best trainers go to unique spots before others. They find rare Pokémon before anyone else.

Pokémon Master

In the game's first month, there were only 142 Pokémon available in the United States. Nick Johnson lived in Brooklyn, New York. He was the first person to catch them all. Because of this, he won a free trip. He got to travel to catch Pokémon that were only available in other countries. Johnson went to Paris, France; Hong Kong, China; and Sydney, Australia.

There are many events that bring Pokémon GO players together. The first one was held in 2017. It was in Charlotte, North Carolina. Niantic called it an experiment. Fans of the game gathered to play Pokémon GO together and explore the city. It went so well that more were planned.

Two months later, a huge event took place in Chicago, Illinois. It was called Pokémon GO Fest. More than 20,000 people attended. So many people were there that they ran into problems. Cell phone service could not keep up. Players needed their cell phones to use the game. There were too many trainers in one area. That made it hard to play the game. Niantic refunded their tickets. But many fans still had fun spending time together. Pokémon GO Fests are now held every year in cities around the world.

DID YOU KNOW?

Friendship ranks were added to Pokémon GO in 2019. Completing an activity in the game with a friend for 90 days straight unlocks Best Friend status.

Pokémon GO Fest draws fans of all ages. In addition to catching Pokémon, they can get special rewards, learn about new challenges, and show their love for their favorite Pokémon characters.

Community Days appeal to young fans, who can have fun catching Pokémon while interacting with other fans of the game in a safe environment.

Community Days are a fun feature of Pokémon GO. Niantic holds these in order to encourage players to join the community. These events happen worldwide. The developers created special items for these days. The Pokémon GO website announces what can be found. "For just a few hours each month, you can encounter a special Pokémon in the wild," the announcement says. "During these hours, there's a chance to learn a previously unavailable move for that Pokémon . . ." These events give trainers a chance to meet other players. Players can even make friends to team up with in the game.

GO Fest Go!

Pokémon GO Fests allow players to meet thousands of other Pokémon GO players. They complete challenges together and unlock unique prizes. They also get to do in-game "research" where they can unlock exclusive loot. These events are a great way for the Pokémon community to come together.

Community Days happen every month. The date is usually in the middle of the month. Many players post their favorite moments on social media. They can tag the official Pokémon GO accounts. This lets other players find these trainers. That helps to make the community even bigger.

Community Days were introduced in 2018. That year featured many unique shiny Pokémon. This means they are different colors than regular Pokémon. Some of these were Pikachu, Dratini, Bulbasaur, and Eevee. Niantic has found ways to keep these Community Days exciting for fans. They have added new ways for players to gain experience points. Experience points make trainers and their Pokémon stronger. Some days have special attacks for Pokémon to learn. These bonuses keep players excited about Pokémon GO.

DID YOU KNOW?

In 2019, Pokémon GO players from 60 countries attended a Pokémon GO Safari Zone event in Montreal, Canada.

Monthly Pokémon GO Community Days are usually held in large parks and other public areas.

Future of Pokémon GO

The Pokémon Company has stayed popular over time. The creators have found ways to make the characters interesting for multiple generations of gamers. Some loved the trading cards. Others preferred the Game Boy games. Now a new generation is playing Pokémon GO. Based on these trends, the Pokémon franchise will stay popular.

DID YOU KNOW?

More than three years after its release, Pokémon GO still makes almost $200,000 in in-game sales per day, seven days a week, 365 days per year!

Pokémon fans can enjoy their favorite characters in books, movies, and even stage performances.

Pokémon GO includes many features from the original Pokémon game and playing cards. These include Poké Balls and all of the original Pokémon characters.

Pokémon GO's developers have worked hard to be **innovative** since the game's creation. This is one reason for the game's continued success. Each year, new Pokémon are introduced. New attacks are also added. The developers have also included some classic features of Pokémon games. Different items from the original Game Boy games were added. This helps the game appeal to traditional Pokémon fans. The game continues to change and challenge its players. The number of fans and players grow every year.

2 Billion Downloads?

In 2019, Pokémon GO reached 1 billion downloads. Many games have the strongest sales right after they are released. Then things slow down. This has not been true for Pokémon GO. The game had a huge growth year in 2018. There was even more growth in 2019. By the end of 2019, the game had earned $2 billion. Users worldwide have increased each year since the game was released. With continued growth, Niantic has its sights set on two billion downloads.

Vaporeon

Niantic is not just looking at the traditions behind Pokémon GO. In the future, they have plans to explore new ways to use AR. A game like Pokémon GO would have been impossible with the technology of the 1990s. AR made this game a reality. The Niantic team thinks there are more possibilities. AR headsets could even be added to the game.

Pokémon GO is already a trendsetting game. The huge popularity of Pokémon GO played a role in the growth of AR. It showed that the technology could be used in different ways. Not many people or businesses were using AR in the early 2010s. Since Pokémon GO, the AR industry is growing. It may make nearly $90 billion in the next few years.

Niantic has many goals for the game. They want to stay responsive. Responsive means adjusting to different situations. Niantic does not want to fall behind. There will be new ideas and new technology. The company wants to use those things as they come along.

DID YOU KNOW?

Augmented reality is being used in the healthcare industry to treat extreme phobias, as well as anxiety and depression.

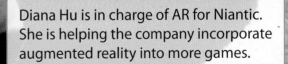

Diana Hu is in charge of AR for Niantic. She is helping the company incorporate augmented reality into more games.

Under the leadership of John Hanke, Pokémon GO and Niantic continue to find success in the gaming world.

Niantic has bought other companies that can help with these goals. One goal is to make Pokémon GO the best game it can be. In 2018, the company bought Matrix Mill. That company helps make AR more accurate. Matrix Mill can help make Pokémon GO a more realistic experience for gamers. Niantic also bought Escher Reality. That company makes games on a larger scale. With Escher Reality, Niantic is creating the Niantic Real World Platform. This would allow users to interact with AR in a more natural way. It would also allow people to experience places in the world beyond their own communities. This concept will make Pokémon GO even more exciting.

Real Competition

In 2018, Jurassic World Alive was released. This AR game copies many of the popular elements of Pokémon GO, but it takes place in the world of dinosaurs. Niantic released a similar AR game for fans of Harry Potter called Wizards Unite. Minecraft Earth, which lets builders explore their creations in the real world, came out in 2019. Many other AR games have been developed following the popularity of Pokémon GO. Gaming experts believe these games could be big competitors for Pokémon GO as developers try to attract fans of AR games with new ideas.

Pokémon GO is a bridge between lovable characters that have been popular for many years and the future of mobile video gaming.

Pokémon GO seemed to become popular overnight. That popularity has stayed strong. Niantic has not announced many specific plans for the future. They do not want to commit to changes. It is hard to say what will happen five years from now. There may be new trends. New technologies may change gaming entirely. The goal is to make Pokémon GO the best game it can be. Niantic has shown they can keep up with these changes. Pokémon GO is sure to find ways for fans to be entertained.

Glossary

augmented reality: adding objects, such as buildings or animals, to the real world using a computer or other device

collaborative: meant to be done together

community: a group of people who live in the same area or who have similar interests

console: a device used for playing video games

franchises: products, including films, books, images, and merchandise, that center around a single character or characters

innovative: a new way of doing something that has never been done before

interactive: allowing users to make choices in order to control something

mobile: able to move around easily

phenomenon: something very unusual or remarkable

virtual: something that appears real but cannot be touched

For More Information

Books

Gifford, Clive, and Anna Brett. *The Ultimate Pokémon Go Handbook.* New York: Stirling Children's Books, 2016. This book is a collection of hints, facts, tips, and other information for both experienced players and new fans of Pokémon Go.

Pokémon Super Deluxe Essential Handbook: The Need-to-Know Stats and Facts on Over 800 Characters. New York: Scholastic, 2018. This book includes almost 500 pages of information on more than 800 Pokémon, including tips for training, battling, and collecting.

Websites

Pokémon GO (https://www.pokemongo.com/en-us/) Niantic's official Pokémon GO website has current information about game changes and updates, as well as tips and tricks for players of all ages.

Why Pokémon GO Is The World's Most Important Game (https://www. forbes.com/sites/jvchamary/2018/02/10/pokemon-go-science-health-benefits/#fc5e0433ab0b) This article discusses the physical and mental health benefits of playing Pokémon GO, including increased exercise and social interaction.

Index

About the Author

Alexander Lowe is a writer who splits his time between Los Angeles and Chicago. He has written children's books about sports, technology, science, and media. He has also done extensive work as a sportswriter and film critic. He loves reading books of any and all kinds.